On the Cross *of* Rejection

D1506930

On the Cross of Rejection

Meditations—when your heart is pierced

Catherine de Hueck Doherty

MADONNA HOUSE PUBLICATIONS
Combermere, Ontario, Canada

Madonna House Publications®
2888 Dafoe Rd
Combermere ON K0J 1L0

www.madonnahouse.org/publications

First Edition

First printing, August 6, 2003 — feast of the Transfiguration of Our Lord

Printed in Canada

Scripture quotations are taken from the New Jerusalem Bible, copyright © 1985 by Darton, Longman & Todd, London, and Doubleday, a division of Random House, Inc., New York.

Edited by Martin Nagy. Parts of this work previously appeared in the book *Doubts, Loneliness, Rejection* by Catherine Doherty, which was published by Madonna House Publications in 1993.

National Library of Canada Cataloguing in Publication Data

Doherty, Catherine de Hueck (née Kolyschkine), 1896–1985
On the cross of rejection : meditations—when your heart is pierced / Catherine de Hueck Doherty.

ISBN 0-921440-91-X

1. Meditations. 2. Spiritual Life—Catholic authors. I. Title.

BT771.3.D633 2003   242   C2003-904426-2

Design by Rob Huston

This book is set in Berkeley Oldstyle, designed by Frederick W. Goudy for the University of California Press in 1938. Headings are set in Balzano, designed by America's famous carver of inscriptions, John Benson.

*What more do we desire
from such a good friend at our side?
Unlike our friends in the world,
he will never abandon us
when we are troubled or distressed.
Blessed is the one who truly loves him
and always keeps him near.*

St. Teresa of Avila

*They will look to the one
whom they have pierced.*

John 19:37

Contents

Introduction

At Mass today, the word "rejection" came to me. It opened its mysterious content some. Beholding it, I cried. Sinner and weakling that I am, it seemed to twist me, tear me apart. I could not help crying. My rejection was so clear, so vivid, so evident.

Rejection is a powerful sledgehammer. We fear rejection so much—first and foremost, emotionally, then, intellectually and spiritually. I suspect that to spiritually accept rejection is a sort of martyrdom.

St. Francis of Assisi went out unafraid. Yet many of his friends and the brethren among the Friars Minor did not approve of him. Do you remember the prayer of St. Francis? "Not to be consoled, but to console; not to be loved, but to love." If he used the word "approve" he could say, "Not to be approved, but to approve." It seems that those who are willing to be ridiculed and disapproved of become saints, and the rest of the company don't. When will we begin to live the gospel without compromise? St. Francis went out unafraid, because, in him, perfect love drove out all fear.[1]

There seem to be gradations of rejection. To be rejected by friends and acquaintances hurts, but less than being rejected by father, mother, brothers, sisters, in a word, family. Parental rejection creates traumas difficult to heal. Rejection by priests, hierarchy, religious is terrible because subconsciously, as well as consciously, such a rejection feels like God's rejection.

Christ was rejected by everybody in varying degrees, all of them terrible. The only ones who followed him to the end, accepted him, shared as much as they could his agony and even death were a handful so small that the sight of it from the height of the cross must have been like gall to him, and yet, at the same time, his only human consolation.

Today, I felt, so very forcefully, the rejections that I've experienced. I have thought that others should be shown their rejection of me. I've puzzled much over this. During Communion, he brought me the answer: "The servant is no greater than the Master. I am the cornerstone, so many rejected me— while I walked the earth and ever since. Is there a love like mine? If I am rejected, why do you complain of rejection?"

This made sense. How deep are the hidden paths of faith—how painful and how deep! In a manner of speaking, Christ was the father and mother, through the mystery of choice, of my misery and poverty. This sharing in Christ's rejection began long ago, and will continue until the end. So I must work now at accepting both, rejection and its child, ejection. I must say a *fiat*.[2]

With the word "rejection" comes the word "defenselessness," which I take to mean that I must not fight this rejection but enter into it as part of the Passion of Christ.

Perhaps it is in atonement for a world that rejects him, too? It is not for me to know why. For me, it is to accept with a mind that understands the agony involved, with a heart smashed by its impact, yet loving, loving, forgiving, and praying constantly for those who reject and eject me out of their lives, hearts, souls, and minds—with a soul bowed down under the weight of it all and emotions seemingly running amuck over it all.

Rejection, defenselessness, if these be your will, your instruments to shape me into your likeness, Beloved, here I am. Speak, your servant hears and with fear, trembling, and a prayer for faith and courage, says, "*Fiat*," Beloved.

Rejection is Surreal

"The stone which the builders rejected
has become the cornerstone;
This is Yahweh's doing,
and we marvel at it.
This is the day which Yahweh has made,
a day for us to rejoice and be glad."

Psalm 118:22–24

Rejection Can Hurt
More Than Any Other Emotion

Rejection can hurt beyond any other state or emotion. To be rejected, not to be accepted, is to enter a dark, tragic garden that appears to be all evil. There is nothing about it that appears to be normal. No, it is all surrealistic.

Not to be accepted, to be obviously and definitely rejected by one's own, is, for those who love God, to enter into Gethsemane.

Jesus went to Gethsemane to pray. He took a few disciples with him. They were overcome with sleep. He knelt by a flat stone, possibly like a table, to pray. A sense of desolation overtook him. He arose and went to those who slept. He looked at them and said, "So you had not the strength to stay awake with me for one hour?" (Matthew 26:40)

He turned back from them. The sense of rejection must have been incredible.

The Son of God felt that even his Father rejected him. He cried out, "My Father, if this cup cannot pass by, but I must drink it, your will be done!" (Matthew 26:42) These words express a sense of total desolation and rejection by man and God. Again, on the cross, he would cry out to his Father, "Abba, Abba, why have you forsaken me?" (Matthew 27:42)

Identify with the Desolate, Rejected Christ

Now, stop right here and try, if you can, by prayer, by identification, by every means at your disposal to identify yourself with the desolate, rejected Christ.

The Garden of Gethsemane is the place where you can share that rejection, and you can say to God (at least I do), "Lord, I am not asleep. I am praying with you right by this stone. I do not reject you. On the contrary, my heart accepts you as the greatest gift that your Father has given us." I do not know if that will console him. But each person, each believer, must speak for himself. This kind of prayer cannot be taught.

When he was led to Golgotha under the weight of his cross, people mocked him. When he was crucified, they continued mocking him. They said, "He saved others; he cannot save himself. He is the king of Israel; let him come down from the cross now, and we will believe in him." (Matthew 27:42)

In the mob that surrounded him, he saw hundreds of people whom his gentleness and kindness had cured and on whom he had lavished his miracles of love. The people to whom he had said, "Your faith has made you whole," were there, also. They rejected him, as if he indeed were the criminal whom the Romans and the Jews said he was.

Crucifixion was thought of as a shameful end to a shameful career. So, the second person of the Most Holy Trinity died between two thieves.

How profound, how deep, how lasting were the wounds of that rejection! Only a little group of women and St. John, the beloved apostle, stood beneath the cross.

Pause for a moment and enter the bitter depths of Christ's rejection—standing side by side with him unto the end, preaching the gospel without compromise, with your very body, mind, heart, and soul, and crying out within, "Lord, I throw my life at your feet and sing that I can bring you such a small thing." At that moment, you will know the joy of rejection.

Lord It Is Good for Us to Be Here

Beloved, I feel like the apostles, "Lord it is good for us to be here." At your feet, I rest in a peace that transcends word and passes understanding. In that peace, thoughts come to me that do not otherwise appear.

I see the world torn away from you. I see the cause of its misery in having denied, rejected your existence, yet yearning for you as never before.

Then, I contemplate my own sins. A lifetime will not be enough to erase them. The enormity of shame makes me shudder. How could I! Beloved, in the light of your presence, their hideousness is revealed in all its clarity. How little I have done for you! How mixed my intentions are! Oh Beloved, above all, have pity on me, have pity on me.

Like a flame, my love for you shoots up straight and clear, overshadowing all the rest. It is exquisite agony to love you, Lord, because it falls so short of what love of you means. Like a prisoner stretching his chains to the breaking point toward freedom, my soul stretches its arms toward you, vainly trying to break away from the shackles of flesh.

Oh Jesus, Son of God, I adore you with all my soul, my mind, my body. I pledge myself to your service in whatever shape you want. I read the writings on the wall. I know that loyalty to you might mean martyrdom. I am only a weak woman but with your Holy Spirit at my side I hope to be strong even unto death.

Jesus, Son of God, I love you with all the love a poor, broken, sinful human heart is capable. I love your poor because you said you are in them. I pledge to dedicate my life to them for your sake. Jesus, Son of God, I believe in you and in all the teachings of your holy spouse the Church. I pledge myself to honor you with her liturgical voice, to obey her unto death—to pray for her, to help her. She will need every little crumb of help.

Jesus Son of God, I am yours now and forever. If in my weakness I fall, lift me up. If I fail, encourage me for I am weak and alone. I love, I believe, I adore your divine will in all things. Amen!

Our Mother's Rejection

"A sword will pierce your soul too—so that the secret thoughts of many may be laid bare."

Luke 2:35

Say "Yes" to God

Long before Jesus went to Gethsemane and stumbled under the weight of the cross, an angel appeared to an unassuming young woman, and prostrating himself before her, he announced to her that she was chosen by God to bear his Son. The angel said, "Hail, full of grace, the Lord is with you," (Luke 1:28) the introduction to the prayer known across the world.

She listened, and then became the example of perfect acceptance of God's will. She listened and said, "You see before you the Lord's servant, let it happen to me as you have said." (Luke 1:38)

Before her child was born, she felt the whip of rejection. Rejection followed almost immediately the disappearance of the angel. When her pregnancy became evident, Joseph, to whom she was engaged, wondered. He could not quite understand. He considered divorce.

Accept God's Mystery

Christ permitted himself to be born in strange, inexplicable circumstances that were a suffering for his mother. Joseph could have accused her of adultery, yet she never justified herself. Before the Son was born, the mother partook of the bitter chalice of rejection and drank it without saying a word in her defense. Then, Joseph had a dream that revealed the facts, and he married her.

After Christ's birth, Mary experienced a great consolation—the coming of the Magi. But rejection overtook her soon again— Herod decided to kill all children the age of her Son.

In a dream, Joseph was told to take her and the child to Egypt. Refugees feel as though both nations reject them. Mary is the Queen of refugees.

She finally returned and led an ordinary life of a wife and a mother. But all the time there was a mystery around her.

After Cana, she went to see Jesus. Her Son said, "Who is my mother? Who are my brothers? Anyone who does the will of my Father in heaven is my brother and sister and mother." (Matthew 12:48–50) How did she feel? She understood the spiritual significance of the teaching. Nonetheless, that seeming rejection must have been hard to bear.

The Sanhedrin rejected Jesus, "Who is he? He is the son of a carpenter. He is a Nazarene. Nothing good comes from Nazareth." This was rejection for Mary, as well.

A Heart Pierced

Mary was truly a marvelous person, sensitive beyond all normal human sensitivity. She was the Seat of Wisdom. How did she make it through the way of the cross, when Christ carried his cross to Golgotha? She watched him fall. She watched his beaten body. She saw that face that had been so dear to her covered with the mud and the dust of the Holy Land.

As Simeon had predicted, she felt the sword pierce her heart. (Luke 2:35) As Jesus fell down amid the jeers and rejection of the people, she was there. She united herself with him. They were always united. What he felt, she felt; she was his mother and, beyond all others, understood who he really is.

When the ordeal was over, they laid him in her arms. She held him fast. I looked hard and long at the Pieta in Rome. How profound was her feeling! He and she were rejected by the mob, by those he had cured and helped. She remembered the words he had said to St. John and her. As she held him in her arms, she must have foreseen, with the wisdom that was hers, the bitter rejection that would come to her Son and to her through the centuries.

He had asked her to be the mother of men. How many of us accept her? How many of us accept her Son? She lives solely for pointing us to the way that leads to her Son. When arms are not outstretched to accept her Son, how bitterly she feels the rejection.

Lord, if this be my last day on earth, I offer it to you with all my love and gratitude. Thank you for having created me—for my parents. Thank you for my vocation. Thank you for the rejection, the pain, the sorrow, the joys. Thank you for every day of my life. Lord, thank you for you.

It Still Hurts

Gratitude swells in me like a surging sea.

Since I have accepted *rejection* my heart is more at peace. Each rejection seems to widen the door of my heart for the Lord to come through. I made my fiat on that, and since then rejections have come to me. It hurts terribly, Lord, but I remember my fiat.

I believe that a Christian is a wounded person, wounded himself out of love for you, piercing wide open his own heart for the world to walk in.

I believe that measures of Christian love are how a Christian loves his enemies, and his patience with himself and others.

I want to run joyously toward you to accept these essential gifts. So Jesus, disregard my complaints. You know they are human. I realize that all these are gifts of your Father, and that they are stepping stones to him. You walked these steps.

But it still hurts.

Suffer for the Sake of Others

"For just as the sufferings of Christ overflow into our lives; so too does the encouragement we receive through Christ. So if we have hardships to undergo, this will contribute to your encouragement and your salvation."

2 Corinthians 1:5–6

Hold Jesus' and Mary's Hands

It is hard to understand how the Lord uses our pain to help others. I wrote a book called *Fragments of My Life*. In it, I touched upon some of my feelings of rejection by certain Christians in both Canada and the United States. Friendship House and Madonna House were built upon my rejection.

Persevering under the constant blows of a whip of rejection can be done only when

Christ and Mary are at your side. Faith alone can continue amid this immolation. The years of rejection follow one after the other like huge stones that are tied about my body. They seem to bring me to the bottom of lakes and rivers. But always, my hands are in the hands of God, of Jesus and Mary. No amount of stones tied around my waist can submerge me.

I, too, now know the joy that the acceptance of pain brings. In Canada, some laity, and some priests and nuns rejected me (never the bishops). In Harlem, my own staff rejected me. A holy Capuchin once said to me, "Catherine, you are getting there. First, you were rejected by the outsiders; now you have been rejected by your own. This is the test that God gives to foundresses."

I turned to him, tears running down my face, and blurted out "Oh, what a terrible thing! Who gives one that sort of thing?"

Calmly, he told me, "God does, Catherine."

Rejection Brings You the Joy of Those Who Have Followed Christ on the Cross

There was another woman who could have cried out just as I did, "From the depths I call to you, Yahweh: Lord, hear my cry." (Psalm 130:1–2) That was Dorothy Day. What that woman suffered in the way of rejection is beyond any ability of mine to put into words. She was rejected by nearly everybody. But she learned the secret of rejection before I did. She was serene and peaceful under the blows of that rejection.

By the way she accepted rejection, she taught me as no one has ever taught me. Dorothy Day and Peter Maurin were the shining lights of the 1930s to whom youth came in thousands to learn the secret of accepting rejections. When she became a pacifist during the war, her houses dwindled. She was crucified in the marketplace. I learned much from Dorothy Day.

Jesus and Mary Love Us So Much That They Want Us to Share in His Passion

I have a couple who write tragic letters to me. Their community has rejected them. They are shunned, not accepted into the circle of their peers. They are wandering like pilgrims, trying to find a place to stay. Rejection is a deep emotion. One cannot get away from the firm hold that emotion has. It appears to grow bigger and bigger and fold a person in its arms. In many ways, it belongs to the psychiatrist. But even with his or her help, rejection remains a profound mystery.

Often, we cannot understand why we or others are rejected. It is so simple. We are rejected, because God loves us, Mary loves us. Jesus and Mary love us so much that Jesus wants us to share in his Passion, for his Passion is his supreme rejection.

If we enter into his Passion, and are ready to be crucified with the nails of rejection, which hurt so much, we will know the joy of Christ. We can make up what is lacking in the sufferings of Christ— "It makes me happy to be suffering for you now, and in my own body to make up all the hardships that still have to be undergone by Christ for the sake of his body, the Church." (Colossians 1:24)—do we remember that?

When we are in pain—physical, psychological, spiritual—we lift our pains into the Lord's cupped hands (the pain of rejection is the hardest). It is like the water that is added to the wine in the sacrament of the Eucharist. The Lord takes our pain, especially the pain of rejection, and he uses it to help others across the whole earth.

Really, we all can say that we know what rejection is. We know because at one time or another we have all experienced it in our bodies and in our minds, but we also know and have experienced the tremendous joy of those who follow Christ on the cross.

We Must Be Holocausts

Somehow, I see clearly that the Parousia[3] depends on us—its coming, I mean—and the realization of this brings me pain, a sort of unutterable pain I cannot express. Christ underwent his Passion for love of us. Now, we who love him, who long for the Parousia must lovingly, eagerly enter his Passion, making it ours.

To hasten the Parousia, we must be holocausts, be the rejected ones.

I must enter deeply into this. I know that, in fact, I am already in it—only, *now*, I must face it fully. Yes, fully and accept it lovingly.

Why Did You Abandon Me?

"Poor and needy as I am,
the Lord has me in mind.
You, my helper,
my Saviour, my God,
do not delay."

Psalm 40:17

We All Experience Darkness

"Father, Father why have you forsaken me?"
(Matthew 27:46) Those words are filled with
mystery and awe. How is it possible that
Christ, the Son of the Father, could say such
tragic things on the cross? And before that,
in Gethsemane, when he begged that the
chalice pass him by? How?

But to my mind, it appears very simple.
Christ was a man like us in all things except

sin. Like any human being, he cried because he was hurting. He said to his Father, "I have really done everything that you want me to do." His humanity asserted itself. I would say that in a moment of stress, he obviously experienced the darkness that we all experience.

We experience our darkness for his sake. The darkness comes to us, and we cry to the same Father, "Father, Father, why have you forsaken me?"

Your Father Hears You Crying

The tragedies of mankind are many. Let us take, for instance, the "boat people" who are Christians. Couldn't they cry out to the Father, "Father, why have you forsaken me?" I think they could.

I think of myself, too, after I left Russia. Once when I was on the Brooklyn Bridge, I wanted to jump, because my life had become meaningless. I held onto the parapet, and I cried, "Father, Father, why have you forsaken me?" My husband was in the hospital. My child was in the home of a stranger. I was earning seven dollars a week. How could I not have cried out to the Father? To whom should have I cried? Only the Father.

Underneath the cross of Christ, a sea of people went back and forth. Many came just to see him dying. The torture of criminals was like a sports event in those days. From his cross, Christ could see that some of those people were ones he had cured. The sight of those he had helped pierced his soul like a sword. Mary had a sword through her soul, so did he. He turned his head a little, and what did he see? Of his apostles, he saw nothing except perhaps the dust that they kicked up in the wake of their flight. Only St. John remained.

The people he had cured rejected him. The apostles rejected him. People yelled, "Let the Christ come down from the cross now, for us to see it and believe." (Mark 15:32) This was blasphemy, of course. There was something to cry about to his Father. And he did. In that tremendous cry of Christ from the cross, the whole of mankind's pain was found.

Jesus' Cry Lifts Us Up to Himself

Dr. Karl Stern used to say to me, "When you deal with emotionally depressed people, try to show them how to unite their depression with the depression of God in Gethsemane."

Jesus arose after prayer and came to his disciples, and they were sound asleep. How would you feel about that? Suppose your friends were asleep when you were in a depression or a terrible bind. He said, "Had you not the strength to stay awake one hour?" (Mark 14:37)

So it is not astonishing that Jesus Christ cried out. In his cry, we take courage because his cry lifts us up to himself. The Father listens to our cry as he listened to the cry of his Son. That Son died, but three days later he arose. Thus, the Father showed how much he loved his Son. It is the same for us.

When we are so absolutely down, we cry, "Father, Father, why have you forsaken me?" The echo of our voice is in our ears.

This echo is something that moves us up the mountain of the Lord very quickly. The Lord stands on the mountain and says, "Friend, come higher," and we are crying to his Father, "Why have you forsaken me?" But if in total trust, and utter faith, hope, and love, we really bend close to the ground and continue to appeal to the Father, our voice becomes lower and lower until it becomes a whisper, until we are silent.

As we move up the mountain of the Lord we suddenly understand what is happening to us—we are entering into the resurrection of Christ.

Why Should I Be Sad?

"I have reared children and brought them up, but they have rebelled against me." (Isaiah 1:2) If this happened to God, why should I be sad? Can I, a mortal, expect less?

Dimly I perceive that the vocation of some Christians is to follow closely in the footsteps of Christ, the Rejected One. If this be so for me, then let me consider it a privilege, a grace beyond compare. I have been selected and called to this vocation, too—not because of my goodness, no; because of God's choice.

"They have gone away backward." (Isaiah 1:4)[4] So it seems. We go away facing, rationalizing—seemingly looking at God—but we 'walk' away from him backwards just the same. *Kyrie Eleison!*

"Your land is desolate." (Isaiah 1:7) Is the land of your soul desolate? It seems that all around the land of souls of humanity is desolate, for many do not follow the real God, even most Christians.

Talk to Someone

"I will certainly not reject anyone who comes to me."

John 6:37

Everyone Feels Rejected

Every human being deeply feels the rejection of his or her fellow man and, quite often, imagines that God also rejects him or her.

Inasmuch as Christ was true man and true God, he felt rejection also. At least, that is my idea of the meaning of his cry on the cross. Being man as well as God, he accepted the sense of rejection experienced by every human being.

A psychiatrist named Jung made a tour of the world analyzing nations and peoples. He concluded that all men feel rejected by God. He found that there was a deep rift at the bottom of men's souls, between them-

selves and that Someone greater than themselves.

Rejection Stems from Guilt

Rejection often stems from imaginary or real
guilt. Various people tend to act differently
when faced with rejection. The English, it is
said, enclose themselves in their so-called
unemotional cape; the French verbalize.
Those who verbalize are often cured from
imaginary rejection.

Consider mortal sin. Mortal sin is an
offense toward God, and the guilt of it, if it is
not verbalized (confessed), is like a cancer
eating up one's heart and soul. When this
happens, it upsets the equilibrium of the
entire person.

Yet, it is better to feel guilty when there
is some reason for guilt. Then, at least, you
can go and verbalize to a priest, or anyone
whom you feel is worthy of your verbaliza-
tion. To feel guilt when there is no reason for
guilt is terrible. Still, the answer to this terrible state is to share what is in your soul, your
heart with someone else.

Confess Your Guilt

We remember that Christ walked the earth. Step by step, walking with him, believing that he is the first person in whom we should confide, we walk with him in faith and in trust, and we tell him our problems.

One should be sharing it with Christ or the Trinity, with our Lady or with the saints, but inasmuch as we are human, it seems that we, also, require a human being to confide in and to talk to. This is called friendship, holy friendship. It leads the other to God. Each being is able to discuss himself or herself to the very depths with the other. If this is not done, the body and soul are poisoned with the eternal poisoning of guilt.

Strange as this might seem, guilt and rejection are almost twin sisters. One has to go to a surgeon to have guilt removed. The surgeon is the priest. He must assuage the guilt. He must allow it to die, slowly but surely, so that the human person can proceed and be receptive to rejection.

Accept Rejection with Joy

When one receives rejection in its pure form, one is accepting that rejection which Christ accepted. That my friends sleep while I pray and am in agony does not affect me. That people call me names causes me to dance. Why? Because Christ was called names— worse ones than I will ever be called.

Thus, rejection accepted in faith is acceptance by Christ. Did you ever think about that? If you accept rejection because you love God, a strange thing happens. God comes down to you—into you—and you begin to feel as if you are walking on air. Why? Because, you chose something much more powerful—your rejection united with Christ's rejection.

In the fusing of the two, you walk directly into the resurrected Christ. In the resurrected Christ, you care little about any rejection. Rejection becomes joy, not sorrow. If you feel a twinge of guilt, you say, "Go away, for I know the resurrected Christ. I am one with that rejection experienced by God."

God the Father says, "I have not rejected you. I have loved you from time immemorial. I have created you out of nothing, and you are mine. I have made you what you are. I, God the Father, shaped you. God the Son died for you. God the Holy Spirit overshadowed you. You are not rejected. You are the friend of my Son, filled with peace and joy. If you have faith, rejection will lie at your feet and then disappear. I will never reject you. Therefore, be at peace. Your face reflects the face of my Son, as well as mine. Rejection is a lie of the devil."

Rejection is a Signpost of Love

You *alone* know how my heart hungers and burns with the desire to love you ever more, know you better "without knowing," so that I can give you to all, especially, to my/our spiritual children.

You taught me that in order to do so I must become a clear channel for you to pass through.

Your feet have walked in mud and dust to me. You are *God* and I am a *sinner*, but I am a sinner, a pauper, a person, a weak one *who loves.* If I truly love and strive to love with an ever-growing fire, then you can and will pass through me.

Love is a fire that burns away dross as it passes. You are that fire. I must be open to only you and fall on your faith as on a sword. This I have understood from loving you, for I have known your mercy.

I have known and still know rejection. Your novitiate in rejection has been thorough. I know it will continue until I die.

Recently, I've begun to glimpse rejection and its meaning in greater depth, and I have shivered at the sight. Only two days ago you showed me why: the people to whom you totally gave yourself unto death have rejected you. How few were in the little group at the foot of your cross! But you *had* to be rejected unto being crucified. You ran toward your final rejection like a lover to his tryst. There could not have been Resurrection unless there was ultimate rejection. For it is through this rejection that death came and through your death, life. Oh Beloved, how you love us!

So I whom you love, and who loves you back passionately, have been given what I prayed for always. In accepting rejection joyfully (in faith), you lead me to the dying on my Golgotha, and my Golgotha is a cross erected before every person I meet. By accepting rejection, I make a road on which you can walk easily to the hearts of people.

All I have to do is be a signpost to you and them. A signpost that you do not need, but want to be there, so that the mystery of love and identification (mine with you) may be present in the world from this rural corner of it.

Childhood Rejection

"I shall not leave you orphans;
I shall come to you."

John 14:18

Being Cradled in a Mother's Arms

A basic kind of rejection so rampant in the world today is childhood rejection.

I am not a psychiatrist, but I know that even the unborn child somehow feels the rejection by its mother. This rejection begins in the womb of the mother—the unwanted baby, whom the mother carries because she has to, not because she wants to, not because she loves the child.

The sound of a baby that has just been born, it seems, is a sound of anger. Birth for the baby is a traumatic experience, because the child dislikes leaving the warm surroundings in which he or she has resided up to then. The parents must assuage this anger.

Did you ever consider the difference between bottle-fed babies and breast-fed babies? One might object, "But the child does not know the difference." Perhaps, but it is a fact that a child who is breast-fed is more peaceful, more quiet, and less subject to feelings of rejection. His anger is assuaged and forgotten because to hold and breast-feed the child, the mother has to cradle him in her arms. A child who is cradled in his mother's arms knows love, or shall we say, that, because of those encircling arms, the child does not know rejection.

In Russia, in the old days, if the mother could not herself provide the milk for her baby, instead of bottle feeding it, she asked a nursing mother to suckle her baby. It was important for her that her baby be cradled in loving arms and suck love through the breast of a woman. Thence came love.

But suppose a baby is bottle-fed and no arms cradle him. He is given a bottle in bed, or in a carriage or stroller. At one time or another, he will feel some kind of rejection in this action. God made women to feed their babies and not to hand them bottles.

Someone to Notice You

In our age of divorces and "shacking up," how does a child feel? I talked to one such child. He was about nine years old. I was sitting on the porch of Madonna House when he came along. He sat down by my side, and he began talking.

"I like it here."

I asked, "Why?"

"Everyone is so kind to me. I feel very happy here."

I said, "That's nice."

He looked at me with big blue eyes and said, "I don't feel happy at home."

I asked, "Why not?"

He said, "Well, here everyone notices me, but at home nobody does. I'm just nobody. My mother seems to look through me. She is nice. She feeds me breakfast, but lunch I get at the school. When I come home there is a woman who gives me some snacks—milk, cookies—but mommy is never home. She has a job, and she is always away, always away. She is never there. She is home on Sunday, but she and my father quarrel a lot on Sunday. Then, they send me to Sunday school. It is all upside down. Everybody here talks about Jesus Christ, but at home nobody does." His words were simple, less stilted than mine.

Then, he put his head on my knees and began to cry. "Can I stay with you forever? I would be so happy here."

Of course, he could not. As I watched the car with him and his parents leaving our yard, I said to myself, "Those parents are laying the groundwork of rejection."

Weeping for Her Children

That little boy made me think. As I thought, I went to our little chapel to pray. I entered into the depths of rejection, a very difficult thing to explain. I saw it as a number of caves along the seashore. Many children were being put into those caves while the parents went to work. In the caves, something happened. The children were seemingly fed and clothed, but, fundamentally, I saw they were deprived of love. I saw the ugly face of rejection, and it cried in the night.

Soon, the sobbing of children overwhelmed me. I no longer saw the caves nor the sea. I just heard sobs, all across the world. Children rejected, children working many hours, children sold into slavery, children sold to pornography. The next thing I knew I was sobbing, too. As I looked into the face of rejection, what else could I do? People did not understand that they were rejecting God. "In so far as you did this to one of the least of these...you did it to me." (Matthew 25:40) "For I tell you that their angels in heaven are continually in the presence of my Father in heaven." (Matthew 18:10)

It seemed that I suddenly heard the voice of God. Did you ever hear, through the gospel, the voice of Christ? "But anyone who is the downfall of one of these little ones who have faith in me would be better drowned in the depths of the sea with a great millstone round his neck. Alas for the world that there should be such causes of falling! Causes of falling indeed there must be, but alas for anyone who provides them!" (Matthew 18:6–7) Can you imagine that? He said it *solemnly.* How many have been rejected!

Everything that we are reaping today—violence, hatred, anger, vandalism among the young—goes back to that strange collective sobbing of children. They don't let anyone know about it, but those of us who love them, hear the sobbing, and we sob with them. Those of us who understand, prostrate ourselves before God and cry for mercy.

Rejected By One's Own

The First Station: Christ is unjustly condemned to death.

As I make the Stations of the Cross in the little church by the river, I feel as if I am before a land of great and infinite beauty. All these years I have walked toward it, and now I stand before its gates, and slowly, oh so slowly, the gates open—not enough to let me in—no, not yet (perhaps never), but enough to catch a glimpse of the infinite beauty within. I know the name of this country. It is *caritas*—love—where all things fall into their places.

Here, all is order, harmony, because all is love, and yet the gates are the gates of suffering and pain. To knock on them, to even start the long journey toward them is difficult and fearsome, because the secret of love, like heaven (which is love), is taken by violence—violence to the self that hates pain, suffering, even unto loss of real love. The First Station is like a first glimpse of the land of love. For here, Love himself sets out on the supreme road of pain and suffering.

It begins with an unjust accusation, for the most painful way of dying to self—the deepest thorns, the heaviest cross, is to be misunderstood *by one's own*, to be rejected by one's own. That is what happened at the First Station.

Christ, my Lord, behold your poor unworthy servant, Catherine, not able to see the connection at first, and then not able to accept it fully. Forgive me, Lord. For though my mind and intellect saw and understood, my heart rebelled and would not let love in. For when I was firmly told, "You are not needed anymore," the world went black before my eyes, and seeking forgetfulness, I blessed the opportunity to come to Combermere. I came here, and slowly, oh so slowly, met the Truth and Love—*you*—waiting for me. How gently, Lord, you showed me your will. How merciful and gracious you have been with me, again.

At the First Station I now know that I must not blame anyone, and what is more, I must both bless them and pray for them, for maybe they knew not what they did; and also because they did what they did through your permission. Who knows but you wanted me here to face myself, and you, in the great silence of pain and of Combermere.

To face, too, many other things: That true poverty is still complete death to self. That humility is the *joyous* acceptance of one's right place before you. That true charity is the emptying of even the residue of the slightest resentment, and the filling of my heart with love for those who threw me out and condemned me unjustly. That there are two processes to this: emptying and filling.

I thank you, Lord, at this your first stop on the *Via Dolorosa*. Teach me its heights, its depths, its breadth, and its lesson of wisdom and love. I am ready, Lord, to listen to your words of life, praying only for the grace of obeying them fully in letter and spirit.

The Door to God's Plan

"Yes, I know what plans I have in mind for you, Yahweh declares, plans for peace, not for disaster, to give you a future and a hope. When you call to me and come and pray to me, I shall listen to you. When you search for me, you will find me; when you search wholeheartedly for me, I shall let you find me."

Jeremiah 29:11–14

God Invites You to Enter a Mystery

Rejection is an immense mystery, one of the many that God places before us. Like all the other mysteries, there is a door and there is a handle. In due time, we are invited to open that door and enter into that mystery.

Sometimes it takes many years before someone faces rejection. It may come in childhood. Sometimes it comes in very early years or during adolescence. It may come in middle age or in old age.

It is a mystery. One is incapable of either apprehending or comprehending it. It has to be entered into. The door must be opened, and we must cross its threshold. Then, we must allow ourselves to follow the intricate paths of its roads, which are sometimes wide and straight, and sometimes twisted and complicated.

The first realization, which will hit us hard, is that we have entered the rejection of Christ. That is why it is a mystery—because Christ entered it, he lived it, he experienced it. Anything that God experienced is a great mystery for all mankind and for each one personally. It is Christ's grace alone that allows us to open that door, to cross the threshold, and to face rejection side by side with Christ.

Let's Face It

Let's face it. He who has been given the grace to follow Christ, who has understood that his heart is in love with God and that he has to follow Christ no matter where he goes, even into the immense mystery of rejection, will find that it will not be easy.

Christ entered that mystery at an early age. His foster father and his mother who were seeking him when he was preaching in the temple at twelve years of age did not understand when he told them that he must be in his Father's house. (Luke 2:49) They did not really reject him, but we hunger so much to be understood by our own. However, he never said anything and was obedient to their wishes until he left his mother's sheltering presence.

As he was gathering his apostles, they followed him. They could not do otherwise, for he who hears the voice of God so intimately in his heart, rises and follows him. They followed him, yes, but many times, they, too, rejected him. Whenever he told them a parable, they wanted it immediately explained.

When he spoke to his disciples about eating his flesh and drinking his blood to have life everlasting, many of them left him completely. (John 6:52–66)

He preached the gospel to the poor, but the poor did not understand, nor did the wealthy.

People were plotting his death. Walking in the shadow of death is a form of rejection.

Over and over again, he opened his mouth and taught the luminous doctrine of the gospel, and each time his own did not understand him and rejected him.

The Sadducees and the Pharisees, the whole Sanhedrin, everyone in power, mocked him and questioned him. They followed him and listened to him for the sole purpose of rejecting every word that he said. Only the simple, the foolish ones, the *humiliati,* the ones who did not seem to matter very much in that society seemed to accept him.

He said, "Foxes have holes and the birds of the air have nests, but the Son of man has nowhere to lay his head." (Matthew 8:20)

Know a Joy that Overcomes Rejection

As we search, a mystery opens up to us. A strange light is shining from it. We enter the mystery, and that which was utterly incomprehensible in the beginning becomes understandable. We swim in it. We are suddenly filled with it. It enters into us, and we enter into it, and we know what we have done. Our swimming ceases, and we simply are permitted to float.

The mystery encompasses us, and we understand that we have chosen to follow Jesus Christ. We have followed him through his pilgrimages, his wanderings across the Holy Land. We now know that we are rejected. We will face the ultimate rejection: Christ occupied one side of the cross. If we decide to follow and taste the bitter cup of rejection, we must be crucified on the other side.

However, long before we are crucified, we will experience that strange feeling of rejection by God the Father. Just like Jesus Christ, we will cry out and say, "Lord, let this chalice pass me by." (Matthew 26:39) Or, if we are already crucified, we will cry out into a day suddenly become dark and frightening, "Father, why have you forsaken me?"

Yes, if we want to know Christ, we must walk with him—not only through his childhood, not only through the desert, not only through his years of preaching, but even further. We have to walk at his side and drink the cup of his rejection.

Our crucifixion will not be of wood, but of sickness, of desertion by those we love, of the death of loved ones, or of a thousand and one possible circumstances that make up a life. Don't you see that if you really want to follow him, there is only one way—you must enter into the mystery of his rejection? Once you have done so, once you have drunk the bitter cup of rejection, then suddenly you will know a joy that overcomes rejection, that annihilates it as if it were not there. Your face will be lifted toward the face of God, and you will sing because of the joy in your heart. Perhaps you will even dance— who can tell?

Those who follow Christ through Gethsemane and Golgotha follow him, also, to the Resurrection. Resurrection is a total renewal. We will have followed him to the end, so then we sit by the lake. He will prepare fish and bread for us, and we will breakfast with him.[5] Then, will our joy be unmarred, and then will we know that in him, through him, with him, we can experience everything that he experienced and come out unscathed.

Save Me, Lord, for I Am Drowning

"From the depths I call to you, Yahweh: Lord, hear my cry." (Psalm 130:1–2)

How often, God, men have repeated these words of the psalmist, each from his or her own depths.

Now I cry out from my depths—or is it from heights? The height of my Golgotha, my crucifixion? I don't know. All I know is that I have to cry out of my depths to you or perish.

Save me, Lord, for I am drowning in a sea composed of a thousand waters that rush into it and create deadly currents that swirl, ebb, and flow around about me, and—as if they had tentacles—try to get hold of me and destroy me.

You alone are my hope. I *trust* in you. I know in my depths that I exist in this sea because of your love, your care, your mercy and compassion. Yet I cannot cease to cry out, for the tentacles are ever close. Take the tentacle of fear—I am afraid of becoming too afraid.

I am afraid of being hurt emotionally, spiritually, intellectually, beyond my human strength to take it. The knowledge, sight, and consequences, after all these years, of no real coalition—of unity, love, joy in you—within the community. All of it slowly adds up to the creation of fear, on all levels of my life.

I dilly-dally with getting up in the morning through fear and also tiredness from not sleeping. My steps lag. This is one face of that fear I have before intolerable pain. It is partly emotional and partly not.

I wonder if it is a temptation. An exaggeration. You who know all things and see all things, tell me, through grace, which is it? You were afraid in Gethsemane. Am I exaggerating the feeling, the realization that I have, that every morning I must face a host of pain-producing reactions, be they emotional, intellectual, temptations from the devil, or whatever?

I am like a leaf blown by your immense and holy wind. Whatever I receive in these unearned graces is for others, not for me.

The pain is intense. I fear that I may in some way dilute or compromise that which you want to make known through me, or do through me, because of the almost craven fear that enters me in the face of rejection or anger.

I cannot convey the fire of your graces and I am sorry about that. The currents and eddies suddenly get hold of me and submerge me into a sea of fears—other fears. I am, it seems, afraid even of going to Mass and of praying the psalms lest (O Lord, forgive my weakness) your awesome light touch me again through them. I am weak, a sinner. I fear, and so I cry, and cry out of my depths.

The Pilgrim

*"Yahweh is near to the broken-hearted,
he helps those whose spirit is crushed."*

Psalm 34:18

Rejection Has Been the Pilgrim Who Walked With Christ

Rejection has a special meaning because it has been, as it were, the pilgrim who walked with Christ. Christ started his pilgrimage, as many pilgrims do, with the desert. Then, he went out from the desert to preach the gospel. All around him, rejection stood as if transfigured. It walked with him, and it sat at his table. It was with him on the terrible day of the cross, from the palace to Golgotha. Rejection walked side by side with him to the cross.

His hands were nailed to wood. The nails hit the soft flesh. As the hammer fastened both hands and feet, rejection arose in all its actuality and manifested itself, for here was God crucified and rejected by men. Rejection is always connected with the rejection of Christ.

We Shall Be Healed

This is something to contemplate, a mystery before which one must prostrate and adore God. It is something to cry about. Yet, at the same time, deep down in our hearts, we know that his rejection is the healing for our rejection.

I am healed by his rejection. Few people who are rejected think of Christ, but they should. From Gethsemane to the cross, and throughout all his life, rejection whispered into his ear. It is not easy to understand the mystery of rejection, because it is so connected with Christ, so deeply ingrained in him, almost a part of him. Still, it is obvious that if you or I place ourselves next to Christ and accept, or at least try to understand, the rejection that he underwent, we shall be healed.

A psychiatrist may help some, but what really can help us is to enter into that immense mystery of Christ's rejection.

Incredible, is it not, that Christ's pain is the healing oil of the Good Samaritan? Prostrate yourself and adore God. Cry about it. Meditate on this often, because in Christ's rejection is our physical and spiritual health.

Light upon the Shadows

I always knew, or long ago sensed the *joy* of Good Friday, for there was that tremendous light of the Resurrection already shining on the cross. I sensed long ago and far away, the shadows of Golgotha on Easter, for they had for a backdrop the blinding light of the Parousia.

A Mirror

"Seek peace with all people, and the holiness without which no one can ever see the Lord. Be careful that no one is deprived of the grace of God and that no root of bitterness should begin to grow and make trouble."

Hebrews 12:14–15

A Thousand Little Pinpricks

Rejection is often like a mirror. It can be part of our examination of conscience. At night I go over my rejections and discover that I have been rejected many times in little ways that don't really amount to much at the moment, but still hurt, even as a tiny pinprick hurts.

Take for instance just saying, "Good morning" or "Good afternoon." We greet someone in the family with these usual greetings, and he or she fails to respond.

This is a type of silence that can hurt us deeply, and yet we cannot say that it is a big thing.

Or, let us consider a mother sitting and resting in the evening. She has worked hard all day for the good of the family, and she is tired. Around her are her teenage daughters. She is sitting there, thinking how nice it would be to have a cup of tea with lemon brought to her. She is tired. Her feet are swollen. She cannot tackle anything more. But not one of her daughters thinks that her mother, who usually makes a cup of tea by herself, needs help to get the tea this time. The mother feels rejected. A pinprick, but how deep is that hurt!

Two girl friends are going to the movies. One is outgoing and dynamic, the other is shy and timid. The latter needs some help from the other who has all the qualities to attract other people, to be somebody. Desperately she hangs on to this friend of hers.

Suddenly, halfway to the theater, that brilliant friend says, "Look, don't bother me so much. Don't hang on me so much. You're a pest."

A few words become a hot flame that sears. In the silence of timidity, the timid one says nothing, but the rejection feels complete. As they approach the theater, she turns and runs away. The brilliant one looks after her, shaking her head. She doesn't realize what she has done.

Little things. The evening comes on slowly. There is a heap of rejection to confront.

Examine Your Conscience

Both the rejected and rejectee, those who are rejected and those who reject them, should make a profound examination of conscience.

Rejecting anyone is a breach of charity, but not only of charity, also of faith. We directly deny, and brazenly, too, the words of Christ, "In so far as you did this to one of the least of these brothers of mine, you did it to me." (Matthew 25:40) There are also his words "Love one another." (John 13:34)

Ponder if you have been rejected during the day, in little ways. The examination of conscience should proceed side by side with memories of those rejections. In the evening, I find that all the tiny pinpricks turn into a larger wound that really hurts. Examining our conscience is very important, because we might be very angry with all those who have rejected us in so many small instances.

The rejected must look deep into their souls, and realize that they should not flee from harsh words nor from pinpricks of rejection throughout the day. On the contrary, they should welcome them, because through them they participate in Christ's rejection.

There is one tremendous truth in all this: that one of the ways Christ saved us was by allowing himself to be rejected by man. Think seriously of that—God came from heaven to save us, and we rejected him.

Rise from the contemplation of your rejections, lift up your hands to heaven, and say to God, "Lord, I want to be rejected too, to share your rejection."

The moment that you have said this, I will hear your laughter, because the joy of God accepting your little sacrifice will transform itself into laughter.

Longing to Do,
Yet Prevented

Beloved, in your great love for us—your desire to save all souls, your untiring efforts to that effect, your utter forgetfulness of self, your opening the gates of heaven, your death on the cross—all the outgrowth of a divine love, you did not command humanity to love you. We have free will.

We can choose or reject your love. We can deliberately prevent the effect of your grace on our souls. Gethsemane was your realization and sorrow of that rejection. This century it will go on like this, one thousand times one thousand or so souls will reject you. Some will try to kill you in the souls of others, even in children.

Beloved, I am a great sinner, but I cannot stand indifferently watching this destruction in the souls of multitudes. Here I am, O Lord, your humblest servant, ready to go and work in your vineyard. I do not ask for honorable tasks. I ask for the hardest, the most thankless, the hidden ones. O Jesus, I love you. Help me to show this love by bringing you souls. Your cry, "I thirst," is before me daily. Let people attribute all possible motives to me. I ask only one thing: that you should know that I love you. I want to console you. I want souls for you—beginning with mine.

A Stranger
in a Strange Land

"Bless your persecutors; never curse them…. Give the same consideration to all others alike. Pay no regard to social standing…. Never pay back evil with evil, but bear in mind the ideals that all regard with respect. As much as possible, and to the utmost of your ability, be at peace with everyone."

Romans 12:14–18

A Heart Pierced

I was rejected by my homeland, Russia, when revolution broke out. Only those who have experienced this kind of rejection can fully understand its immense power and its infinite tragedy. The revolution rejected the so-called aristocracy, the establishment, and hunted down the opposition. Today I read about South Africa and other countries where people are killed by the thousands. I think of Russia. Ten million refugees left Russia. The number of people killed before and after Stalin took power ran into tens of millions.

One leaves his country. If not, he dies. He flees the fatherland, the one he loves, that means so much to him. He was born there. He absorbed everything about its customs and ways. All of the sudden, he is compelled to enter a strange and foreign world. He saves himself. He becomes a refugee.

I think I can comprehend something of what Our Lady felt when her Son was killed. I had to witness the killing of many Russian sons, of my Russian brothers, many fathers and mothers. The sword Simeon spoke of penetrated Russia.

The country might have been wonderful to us, but it was no longer our own. We became strangers in a strange land.

Jesus Was a Refugee

Our rejection shook us. It permeated our nights, filled our dreams and our conversations. Often, we gathered some place where Russian was spoken and recalled the days of old.

At such moments, one remembers that Jesus was a refugee. So were his mother and foster father. In faith, one plunges into the exile of Jesus from his land into the land of Egypt. Our exile from our land, then, becomes more understandable. We refugees are making up what is wanting in the sufferings of Christ. (Colossians 1:24) St. Paul's words are a mystery that refugees probe.

Then, there are the Jews, rejected by everyone; a strange nation rejected for centuries through the ignorance of mankind. When you consider them, something deep and profound comes from your heart. To be rejected by the majority of mankind must be terrible.

I recall my father talking about this. He often opened his doors to Jews who were victims of this rejection. He used to say to me, and our family, "Always be kind to the Jews, because they are the rejected ones. Don't ever forget that out of their bosom came Jesus Christ, Mary the Mother of God, and the Apostles."

The Persistence of Anger

When you face Auschwitz, words fail. The Nazis not only rejected the Jews, but made martyrs out of them. The Jews believed in one God, Yahweh, and they were made martyrs for that belief. Their martyrdom earned them the land of their forefathers.

The Jewish people in turn are rejecting the Arabs. A pain comes into your heart when two Semitic people feud with one another. There should be room for both in that ancient land.

If you have strength to open your eyes and look across the world, what do you see? In almost every nation, you see rejection in one form or another. Much rejection is motivated by anger. It becomes impossible to open your eyes, because there are few countries where this ultimate, cataclysmic rejection is not operative. This incomprehensible rejection begins to overwhelm you.

After witnessing such rejection, we have to stand at the side of Christ, take his hand, and say, "Lord, have mercy on us. We have sinned. We have substituted

hatred for love. The love that you gave us as your last commandment[6] has been turned into hate. Have mercy on us, Lord."

I Thirst

Dear Jesus, you said seven words on the cross and as I ponder over them, one stands out to me: "I thirst." (John 19:28) You thirst for souls, for those souls whom you see in the future—that future that for you is always the present.

You saw each of those billions of men, women, and children pass before you, for whom you endured all those tortures. As a beggar, you addressed to each one of us these words, "I thirst," for all of us had passed before your cross. We could not avoid it. It was everywhere: on our churches, in our rooms, on our graves. On that cross you hung, and daily, hourly, you repeated, "I thirst."

Look into each soul you looked at, into every eye you once met. Some have seen you and yet saw you not; heard you, yet heard you not, for they were busy with their own business. They had gotten so used to seeing you crucified everywhere, they did not even stop but rushed by. Others stopped, with hatred. Their sacrilegious hands reached out and overthrew your cross and you. They trampled you under their feet, renewing your agony. They rejected your thirst and proclaimed you had no place in their homes. In their countries they forbade your emblem, and killed and exiled your servants.

Others, in their fury at your words "I thirst," went further. They destroyed your temples, forbade your worship—and, dear Lord, dared to take you away from children so that these little ones would never hear the name of the one who loves them so much.

You saw all this, my Lord, when from the height of Calvary you said, "I thirst."

O Lord, grant that I not be deaf to your word. Here is my soul, O Lord, for you to quench your thirst. Allow me to give it to you.

Your thirst was not for water, cool and limpid as it might have been. It was for the soul, for the coolness of a loving touch. Your thirst for love, incomprehensible as it is, is for the love of the children of man.

When you looked at the world from Calvary, you had the consolation of seeing your Blessed Mother, Mary Magdalene, St. John, and the good thief; and gazing across the centuries, you saw the army of virgins and holy widows, of priests and monks, and simple, ordinary people whose lives were given to your service. You saw a multitude of sinners—who heard your lamentation, "I thirst"—suddenly leave the table of iniquity, and follow you to the end. You saved the sinner. You died for us.

O Lord, do not permit me to tarry a moment, now that I have heard your cry. Allow me, the greatest sinner of all, to answer it and to spend the rest of my life trying to quench your thirst for souls by offering you wine and emptying myself to bring you others.

Offer the Other Cheek

"Offer no resistance to the wicked. On the contrary, if anyone hits you on the right cheek, offer him the other as well."

Matthew 5:39

Flaming Faith

I witnessed once "the power of meekness."

During the early days of Friendship House in Toronto, I was returning on an evening to Friendship House. I came across a preacher holding his pitch at the corner of a slummy street surrounded by a large audience of the poorest people, especially the Brothers Christopher who were so plentiful, then. These were the depression years, and folks had little to do but hang around the corners of streets listening to anyone who wanted to talk to them.

Always interested in anyone speaking of God and the things of God, I stopped to listen. I liked what I heard. This evangelical preacher was talking, of all things, about *caritas* (love) and *pax* (peace)—talking forcibly, with a flaming faith.

Among his audience was a hulking brute of a man slightly worse for liquor but not drunk. He interrupted the preacher and started abusing him in no uncertain terms.

The preacher, a slight man, standing on a soapbox, went on preaching. His voice got gentler. A little kind smile touched his eyes and lips, and gave a lovely light to his otherwise plain face.

The big man got angry. He opened the palm of his hand and gave a resounding smack with his open palm to the cheek of the preacher. The big man hit hard. The preacher fell from the soapbox onto the dirty pavement.

The Other Cheek

The fall must have hurt the preacher, for he got up painfully. Slowly, he got back on his box. His face was dirty from the pavement, slightly bloody, and with a big red spot on his cheek from the slap. He smiled gently, again, a real loving smile. You knew he meant it.

He turned his other cheek to the big man saying, "Brother, here is my other cheek, for I love you in the Lord, and I love the Lord, and he said to turn the other cheek to him who smites you. So here is my other cheek."

The Power of Meekness

There was a dead silence for a spell.

The big man suddenly crumpled and fell to his knees before the preacher, weeping bitterly. I felt a shiver going down my spine, for I was witnessing the *terribilis*[7] power of meekness that the Lord Christ spoke about.

As I looked over the faces of the motley audience, I saw many who were wiping tears furtively from their eyes, mostly with the back of their hands or with their dirty sleeves.

That night, the preacher reaped a great harvest for the Lord.

We must open ourselves in peace and in love and without fear, defenselessly, to all hostilities of all people—in all senses, including the emotional. I know that I must. Not defending myself by a thousand tricks, but lovingly open myself, even unto my subconscious, and then perhaps my subconscious will be cleared of all its undergrowth by Christ the Lamb.

The Poverty of Forgiveness

Rejection is one way of practicing the great gospel virtue of poverty. I desire rejection with my whole heart. This is when poverty becomes rich, totally and graciously rich, bedecked in those marvelous garments that St. Francis of Assisi thought of when he spoke about "Lady Poverty."

The remnants of true poverty will clothe us. We will be resplendent, because we have reached a point where surrender to God in speech, surrender to God in deed, has reached its heights. Now we know that poverty contains the forgiveness of rejection. That is a tough one. But if you want to embrace the gospel virtue of poverty, there it is for you: to accept smilingly all the rejection heaped upon you—smilingly, because you follow the footsteps of Christ.

It is a totality of poverty that embraces all aspects, including physical and spiritual. When you accept it, you will stand as a witness before the world, a witness to the tragedy of the rich, a witness to the misery of the poor, and a witness to the God of the poor.

The poverty of forgiveness not only becomes a door to God's heart, but a cradle to his infancy. Kneeling down, arms aside, a heart wounded by a lance—that is a door to God. Poverty becomes a manger for the Christ child to rest in. There is Lady Poverty in all her beauty. Follow Jesus Christ. See his rejection again and again. Come to the crucifix.

Defenselessness

"This, in fact, is what you were called to do, because Christ suffered for you and left an example for you to follow in his steps. He had done nothing wrong, and had spoken no deceit. He was insulted and did not retaliate with insults; when he was suffering he made no threats but put his trust in the upright judge. He was bearing our sins in his own body on the cross, so that we might die to our sins and live for uprightness; through his bruises you have been healed. You had gone astray like sheep but now you have returned to the shepherd and guardian of your souls."

1 Peter 2:20–25

Words of God

Two little words came to me during Mass at different times and on different days: *meekness* and *rejection*. Words dealing with God in any fashion have great depths but do not open themselves at once to those who seek their full meaning. Like all the things of God and ways of God, they open the doors to their beauty, to their full sense, as it were, slowly, gently, to those who persevere.

At first glance, *meekness* and *rejection* seemed to have little to tie them together. But as days went by, as I thought them over, examined them, tried to enter into their depths, a pattern emerged, a pattern in which those words grew, entwined themselves around each other, then separated and came together again.

Meekness

I have often meditated on meekness in the past years of my life. It is a virtue that has attracted me. I loved the beatitudes. Meekness prominently figures into them. The Lord said that the meek shall inherit the earth. (Matthew 5:4) He also says to me, "Learn of me. I am meek and humble of heart." (Matthew 11:29)

But up to now, all my meditations on that beautiful and gentle and strong word dealt with *non-retaliation*. Somehow they went together with the words of Our Lord, "If anyone hits you on the right cheek, offer him the other as well." (Matthew 5:39) I connected that word with Dorothy Day, the Quakers, the pacifists.

But as I meditated on that word, another word came to show me its depths: *defenselessness*. On the screen of my mind, I saw the defenseless Christ during his Passion, for it is said that he was led defenseless like a lamb to the slaughter. (Acts 8:32) I found out that meekness and defenselessness go together. But what did it mean to me personally? I continued day after day to meditate on this matter.

Defending Ourselves

We are always on the defensive—you and I, and most of the world. We always have our guards up. Always have shields and bucklers and masks not of the Lord's making, but our own, to protect ourselves from real or imaginary threats or attacks.

Ours is a century of neurosis and psychosis. The Christians of the world for about 400 years or so have been drifting away from God until finally, they cut themselves off from him officially and completely by becoming atheists. Men without God perforce become neurotic and psychotic. Around them and from them begin to stem the fruits of the devil—fear, confusion, insecurity. As the atheists grow, the devil incarnates himself further and further, letting the stench of all that is evil spread itself, as it were, in ever-widening circles of eddies, until all men—even the good ones, the believing ones—are affected in one way or another.

Because of this tragic situation of the world's soul, all of us are somewhat confused. All of us are afraid of threats and attacks from the atom bomb or our next-door neighbor. Take me, for instance, I too am on the defensive, emotionally speaking. At times I would not take time to listen but would rush in, seemingly impatient, and proceed to solve, or think I solved, problems. This didn't happen always, but sometimes it did.

Well, today I know why I did that. I was defending myself against hostility. I was exhausted, humanly speaking, from the constant waves of hostility that even now, like big waves, beat constantly at the shores of my person. It didn't matter that I understood that I was only a symbol.

I certainly was not defenseless. I defended myself on such occasions. Defended myself unconsciously or semi-consciously. But today, with my new insights into meekness and its gentle attribute, defenselessness, I understand better.

Blending Ourselves with Christ

What you and I must do is become defenseless and blend ourselves with Christ the Lamb, allow ourselves to be led to the thousand slaughters that will fill our lives—be defenseless and thus be meek—as he was meek and defenseless.

Humbly, as is the way of my people in Lent, I bow low before people and ask them to forgive me for all the defenses that in the past I have put up against them in any way.

In faith and love, and trusting in the grace of God, I certainly will do the impossible to not put any defenses, emotional or otherwise, against others in the future.

We must not justify ourselves when unjustly accused. That is part of the defenselessness of Christ. A slight meditation on meekness brings forth, not only non-retaliation, "Vengeance is mine—I will pay them back" (Romans 12:19) but also love of enemies, and then goes deeper and deeper to bring a holy defense-lessness that strengthens us and brings peace to those who attack us.

Being Stripped

The stripping is yours, Beloved. I see it as your gift, you wish me to be stripped and cleansed, *kenotic*, emptied, before your mother clads me in my wedding garments on my death bed.

You have stripped me in a measure even as you have been stripped, for you loved me much through persecution and misunderstandings. You bathed me in a sea of pain which alone truly washes away selfishness. I thank you for all of this.

You will me, I know, to walk alone in this darkness. You hold everyone's eyes and none see the depth of my agony.

I understand, in my darkness, and I accept it. You walk with me, then, although I know it only in an opaque darkness of faith.

To make this faith grow, you placed me in this stripping. Thank you, Lord. But help me to stay in it, for without you I can do nothing.

Here it is, Beloved, I give the gifts of your love back to you, thanking you for filling my empty hands for that purpose.

Stripping follows me, dwells with me wherever I go, Alleluia!

I know that you will continue to strip me until I die. Alleluia!

I only cry to you for the grace and strength to stand still under your loving hands while you strip me.

The Heart of a Child

"In truth I tell you, unless you change and become like little children you will never enter the kingdom of Heaven. And so, the one who makes himself as little as this little child is the greatest in the kingdom of Heaven."

Matthew 18:2–4

More Than Psychology

During Communion, the Lord, as it were, sent me a word to think about. What has the word "rejection," which seems to belong to the textbooks of psychiatry, to do with God and me and meditation and Lent? I confess it puzzled me for quite a while.

Friday is a prayer day for me in my desert or "poustinia" as the Russians call the desert. On a Friday, in the great silence of the Lord in my cabin, I began to see light.

Rejection belongs to the Passion of Christ. In fact, it belongs to his whole life.

Rejection Belongs to Christ

Let's briefly look at how rejection belongs to Christ's life.

When St. Joseph found out that his betrothed was pregnant and he had not known her, he would have divorced her were it not for the angel's message. Rejection of Mary, full of grace, meant rejection of the fruit of her womb, Jesus.

The innkeepers in Bethlehem rejected the Holy Family, including the unborn Christ, in shelter and hospitality.

The Pharisees and Sadducees—the Old Testament priests and the learned ones—rejected Christ, with the exception of one or two. That must have been a terrible pain to Christ, the human. (Of course, Christ, God, knew about it before hand).

When he went to his hometown, Nazareth, the people tried to stone him, not believing or accepting the son of Joseph, the carpenter.

One day when he proclaimed that he was the bread of life, that unless we ate his flesh and drank his blood we would not have life everlasting, most of his followers, who used to walk with him, rejected him publicly and in a group saying, "This is intolerable language. How could anyone accept it?" (John 6:60)

Phillip rejected Christ and his words, partially or totally, by asking thoughtless questions, as so many of us do. It seems to me that Christ was touched to the quick by this non-accepting attitude from his beloved disciple; he scolded him. The rejection of Peter made him sad. What Judas' rejection—sealed with a lying kiss—did to Jesus, only the Father knew.

From the time that he was arrested in the Garden of Olives to the time he was nailed to the cross and hanged from it, rejection followed him step by step. Wherever he went—among the servants of the high priest, those surrounding Pilate, and the mob (his own Jewish people) who violently yelled, "Crucify him"—he was rejected by those he had helped or instructed.

From the height of his cross, the rejection must have been most evident. How many familiar faces did he see among those who were laughing at and taunting him? Perhaps some of them had seen the resurrection of Lazarus and other miracles he performed.

Stop and think of the rejection from his very own, his beloved apostles with whom he had walked three years, to whom he had given himself so unstintingly. There was only one apostle in the small group under his cross. Judas was dead, but where were the other ten?

Remember the rejection that tore from his parched, pain-filled mouth and lips, those terrible words, "Father, Father, why have you forsaken me?"

Rejection, like pain and loneliness, were the shadowy companions of his whole Passion, perhaps his whole life.

Christ Went There Before You

Rejection is a word that I have to meditate on indeed, if I want to enter the Passion of my Beloved. I saw the tremendous love of Christ under a new light. He was in every way and in everything but sin, a man like you and I. He knew and experienced all that we in our humanity have to know and experience of pain and of sorrow. It stood to reason that he would experience the feelings of rejection in order to help us to understand, bear, and overcome that terrible feeling of rejection— so neurotic, so emotional, so deadly, so life shattering.

Christ is the high priest, the great teacher, the great physician, and also the great psychiatrist, who touches us, enlightens us, and heals us—not by psychiatric sessions as human psychiatrists have to do, but via a love, an empathy that identifies itself with us. A brief perusal of the gospels shows us how he was often rejected by people and how he dealt with it.

Fear of Rejection

Most problems, on the emotional side, have to deal with that mind-searing, soul-searing violent emotional threat that makes us sick with so many psychosomatic symptoms. They can be summed up in *fear of rejection*.

To put it another way, we seek approval by the person that matters and by others, too. We crave and hunger for it, because we equate it with love, infantile or otherwise. Rejection almost equates death to us, a sort of living death, filled with loneliness. For non-acceptance, another way of saying rejection, spells aloneness, pain, sadness, and being unloved—in effect, a living death, or hell on earth.

We are on the defensive constantly. We are afraid to reveal our true selves. We are abysmally frightened to be open, to trust, to communicate lest perchance people that matter will find out *our true selves and reject us*. With this fear come feelings of inadequacy. Being afraid of rejection, we are unable to see ourselves as we are, accept ourselves as we are. We are unable to love ourselves first, so that we may be capable of loving others.

"Where do these wars and battles between yourselves first start? Is it not precisely in the desires fighting inside your own selves?" (James 4:1)

Thus, the feeling and fear of rejection, and the putting up of defenses constantly puts us in a straightjacket, a prison of fear and a thousand other emotions. We are half alive in the reality of living, unable to love, yet longing to be loved and accepted. Gently, Christ comes to our rescue.

The Heart of a Child

He comes with two words—*meekness and rejection*—showing us, I think, that if we are truly meek, we shall be defenseless, unfenced, open. A defenseless person is a trusting person, a meek person, a person full of faith with a heart like a child—of whom is the kingdom of heaven.

Defenseless people are open to all pains and all thrusts of the knives of other people's words, glances, and deeds, *because they are strong in faith and strong in love,* because they don't retaliate, don't defend themselves. In a word, they are "meek." They are not hurt, for the knives (such as harsh words and deeds) bounce off that *terribilis* shield and buckler of theirs, the one fashioned by faith, and fall at the feet of the attacker and the attacked.

From their hearts and souls stream light almost unbearable for they are truly Christlike. The light of Christ shines for them, unimpeded, and envelopes the attacker with its gentle love, illuminates his soul, and heals him.

The meek, defenseless persons who practice this virtue for Christ's sake and love's sake will never feel rejected, because they are anchored in Christ through every step of his rejection. They have heard and seen how love itself dealt with rejection— meekly, forgivingly, lovingly. They do likewise and if they ever were neurotics, by being anchored in Christ's rejection, they are healed and heal others.

Lovingly I pray that the humble and rejected Christ may, in his Sacred Heart and in his love, make you meek, defenseless and, hence, secure against any rejections.

Desire to Be Loved

The last few days have had much darkness. I encountered sullenness, unfriendliness, suspicion, gossip and soul-searing viciousness. How strange it seemed! How far removed from all I love, appreciate, and, in the natural order, would choose. My heart desired so much to be loved, but this love was denied me. Always I worked in pain, darkness, and sorrow.

Thus ran my thoughts as I sat crocheting and reflecting. It seemed to me at the moment that until then I had not yet felt the full depth of loneliness, had not drank such a bitter chalice. Darkness—stygian—closed in on me. Then in that darkness, faintly the eyes of my soul saw Gethsemane and Golgotha, and I knew why it was all thus. I knew that for those who try to love him who died just for love of such people, there was no other way but the way of rejection, of pain, of seeming utter and terrible crucifixion.

Lord, I too cry from these depths, "Let it be done in me according to thy will. Alleluia!" This, too, for the work of love.

Why Are We
Afraid of Ridicule?

"In love there is no room for fear,
but perfect love drives out fear."

1 John 4:18

I'm in Love

Most people are afraid to express themselves lest they be ridiculed. The Bible says that perfect love casts out fear. If we are in love with God, why should we be afraid of ridicule?

I was sorting holy cards, and I thought, "Jesus was buffeted, hit on the face, tortured, and, especially, ridiculed. When he got to the Roman palace, the soldiers bowed and said, 'You are the King of the Jews,' and they ridiculed him."

Ridicule is one thing that makes people sort of shut up and go inside of themselves. They sit there and look to the left and to the right, worrying, "What is she thinking? What is he thinking about what I say?" If you are a Christian, remember that we follow a God who has been ridiculed.

I'm a Fool in Love

Brother Juniper, a friend of St. Francis of Assisi, used to seesaw. The kids laughed at him, and adults did, too, to see a man playing on a seesaw, up and down, up and down, up and down. He tried to be foolish for Christ's sake, because Christ said to St. Francis, "I want you to be a fool and a simpleton, the likes of which have never been seen." To be a fool for Christ is to expect to expose yourself to ridicule.

We are afraid to step out of line. If the fashion is miniskirts, we wear miniskirts. If beards are "in," we wear beards. If people wear long hair, we wear long hair. If maxi skirts are in vogue, we wear maxi skirts. Why do I have to do what X, Y, and Z do? I am a human being. I don't have to follow the crowd.

We are afraid of being unapproved. We need approval as we need air. We go haywire if we are not approved of, by whomever. How many approved of Christ in his life?

What is it for me that demands so much approval? Emotions. I don't think we put our roots in Christ. All over the place people are not approved of, but somehow or other, they survive. Do you remember the prayer of St. Francis? "Not to be consoled, but to console; not to be loved, but to love." St. Francis went out unafraid, because in him perfect love cast out all fear. Many of his friends and his brethren of the Friars Minor did not approve of him, but he is a great saint. There's a book called *Holy Indifference*. If we felt indifferent, life would be easy—or rather, both hard and easy. It takes some time to live this out.

We have a lousy yardstick about ourselves that adds to all this misery—the wrong image of ourselves. What is it that we measure ourselves by? Production. But, our true measure is Jesus Christ—his incarnation, life, death, and resurrection. You are precious.

Stop and think what Christ paid for us. You mustn't think only of Christ dying for "mankind." He did, but "mankind" is a sort of amorphous word. If you were alone, he would have died for you, because he loves you. When we consider what price Christ paid for us, to measure ourselves by production is a prostitution of ourselves.

We are afraid to stand out, but that is what God wants us to do. "Anyone who is not with me," he said, "is against me." (Luke 11:23) To be with him is to stand out from the crowd. It is to be subject to ridicule. It is to be different. It is to have a different attitude to the price of who we are, not production-minded, but God-minded, God-saved.

Forgive Others—Forgive Yourself

All those fears get together, and we have them all. As I thought about this, it seemed impossible to do anything else but kneel down and pray for all those who are afraid, because fears ruin human health and take people away from God. We have tragedy upon tragedy, because we are afraid.

I simply knelt down and started praying to the Father, for the Son said, "The Father will give you anything you ask him in my name." (John 15:16) I am not ashamed to say that I cried out to the Father to take those fears from us, especially, from the young ones and the ones who are struggling to live the Christian life, the gospel without compromise. I felt so compassionate, so tender towards you.

In those books on the healing of memories, what are the memories that have to be healed? The majority of the memory is that father and mother did not approve of me, or they didn't love me enough, and then you go down the line. What are all those memories? If we just brought them forth and entered into bringing them forth without fear, they soon would evaporate, because fear is a weapon of the devil, one way or the other.

Two things exorcise fear. One is prayer, and the other is forgiveness of those who have done us harm. Forgive parents and relatives or whoever has hurt us, but perhaps we should start by forgiving ourselves. The person that each of us must forgive is our own selves; you must forgive yourself.

Be kind to yourself, for you are your first neighbor.

Start forgiving yourself. If you really forgive yourself you will have peace, the peace that surpasses understanding.

The Sweet Savor of Poverty

I am truly beginning to feel unsubstantial, as if I were not there. Rejections follow rejections, small little ones, weaving a crown of thorns that seems to hurt as much as big rejections.

Yet, together with the never-absent pain, there is also a great joy, because at long last, I am beginning to get a real taste of poverty. The poverty I always talk about. For I am poor, now, in the true sense of that deep word.

That is, I am beginning to be poor, just beginning, and for this I am thankful, Lord. I truly am. I pray, though, that I may enter this poverty with humility, which is truth, and accept it gracefully.

Beloved, I thank you for everything, everyone, and every day.

Afterword

My mind and soul are still filled with the question of the silence of God. I have to enter God's silence. I have understood a little what this entering into his silence means. To me, as perhaps to other Russians, it means "folding the wings of the intellect" and placing them into the heart. It means entering a phase of repose, allowing cares, thoughts, tensions to fall off one's mind, heart and soul as one lets one's garments fall, and then waiting in peace and quiet for the Lord to come and act—or act and come. Such has been my little knowledge of the silence of God in which the Holy Spirit works.

But now, something else has been added. It seems to me as if I stand before an abyss. On the other side is Christ—Christ, the Rejected One. To me, his rejection is epitomized on the balcony of Pilate when, dressed in purple, wearing a crown of thorns and holding a scepter, he is presented to the populace.

Although I desire beyond desire to cross the abyss (even though I am in fear of doing so), it seems as if the only way I can reach the Rejected Christ is to become one with all the rejected ones—and that means becoming one with humanity.

Then, I shall become one with him and enter his silence. The great silence of Love, which heals, comforts, gives strength. There and only there will I know, truly know, Love, as in God. Then and only then, will I be able to love, to heal, to help, as I so terribly desire to do. I, too, am so deeply one of the rejected.

But I have to do more. I have to enter the tunnel in people's souls, minds, and hearts, and lift—lift up, up, up their sins and hostilities; and lift up, up, up their rejections and other suffering to God.

Thank you for listening.

Endnotes

1. "In love there is no room for fear, but perfect love drives out fear." (1 John 4:18)

2. *Fiat* is Latin for "let it be done." Catherine is referring to Mary's words, "You see before you the Lord's servant, let it happen to me as you have said." (Luke 1:38)

3. The second coming of Jesus.

4. King James Version. The New Jerusalem version reads, "They have turned away from him."

5. See John 21:9–13.

6. "I give you a new commandment: love one another; just as I have loved you, you also must love one another." (John 13:34)

7. *Terribilis* is the Latin root of "terrible."

MADONNA HOUSE PUBLICATIONS
COMBERMERE • ONTARIO • CANADA • K0J 1L0

"Lord, give bread to the hungry, and hunger for you to those who have bread," was a favourite prayer of our foundress, Catherine Doherty. At Madonna House Publications, we strive to satisfy the spiritual hunger for God in our modern world with the timeless words of the Gospel message.

Faithful to the teachings of the Catholic Church and its magisterium, Madonna House Publications is a non-profit apostolate dedicated to publishing high quality and easily accessible books, audiobooks, videos and music. We pray our publications will awaken and deepen in our readers an experience of Jesus' love in the most simple and ordinary facets of everyday life.

Your generosity can help Madonna House Publications provide the poor around the world with editions of important spiritual works containing the enduring wisdom of the Gospel message. If you would like to help, please send your contribution to the address below. We also welcome your questions and comments. May God bless you for your participation in this apostolate.

Madonna House Publications
2888 Dafoe Rd
Combermere ON   K0J 1L0
Canada

Internet: www.madonnahouse.org/publications

E-mail: publications@madonnahouse.org

Telephone: (613) 756-3728